Piano • Vocal • Guitar

THE VERY BEST OF
Lee Greenwood

contents

A *J. Aaron Brown & Associates* Publication
in association with

HAL LEONARD
PUBLISHING
CORPORATION

Home Office: National Sales Office:
960 East Mark Street   8112 West Bluemound Road
Winona MN 55987   Milwaukee WI 53213

ISBN-0-88188-436-7

AIN'T NO TRICK
(It Takes Magic)

Words and Music by
STEVE PIPPIN and JIM HURT

Moderately, with an even beat

Ain't no big deal ___ to lose, ___
It's just part of ___ the game, ___

I keep tell-in' ___ my - self. ___
I keep tell-in' ___ my - self. ___

I get used to the blues, ___   I won't stay
Hard luck found out ___ my name, ___   I let my

DIXIE ROAD

Words and Music by MARY ANN KENNEDY,
PAM ROSE and DON GOODMAN

Moderate half time ♩ = 96

1. I would pick, and we would sing to the rhy-thm of that front porch swing; the

moon-light was a spot-light that we shared. I found new

notes on that old gui-tar; she be-lieved I could be a star. She

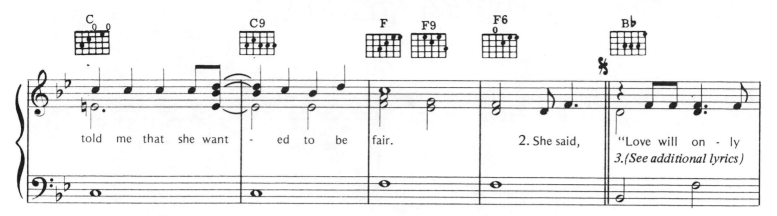

told me that she want - ed to be fair. 2. She said, "Love will on - ly
3.(See additional lyrics)

hold you down. Boy, you're glo - ry bound, ___ and we can't share a world ___

___ of dif-f'rent dreams." So, I chased mine, ___ and she found ___

___ hers, too, but some-one else ___ made hers come true. ___ Now I'm a star, ___ but

Chorus:

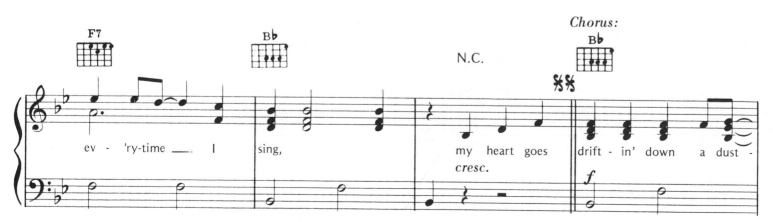

ev - 'ry-time ___ I sing, my heart goes drift - in' down a dust -

Verse 3:
Ev'ry night I'm in a diff'rent place,
And I search in ev'ry stranger's face,
Tryin' to find a girl who's just not there.
She's back there in Montgomery,
And I'm clear across the country,
But whenever I'm alone, I go back there.

FOOL'S GOLD

Words and Music by TIMMY TAPPAN
and DON ROTH

DON'T UNDERESTIMATE MY LOVE FOR YOU

Words and Music by DAVE LOGGINS,
STEVE DIAMOND and STEVE DORFF

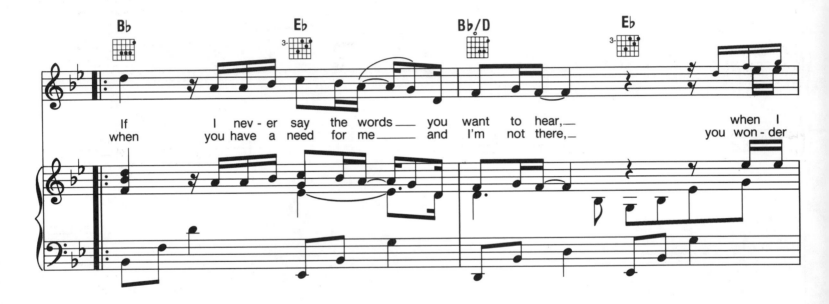

If I nev-er say the words you want to hear,
when you have a need for me and I'm not there,
when I you won-der

hold you near may-be they get said an-oth-er way.
if I'm where I could meet some-one who'll take me from you.
A

GOD BLESS THE U.S.A.

Words and Music by LEE GREENWOOD

thank my luck-y stars to be liv-in' here to-day, 'cause the

flag still stands for free-dom and they can't take that a-way._____ And I'm

Chorus

proud to be an A-mer-i-can___ where at least I know I'm free. And I

won't for-get the men who died, who gave that right to me. And I'd glad-ly

stand up; next to you and de-fend her still to-day. 'Cause there

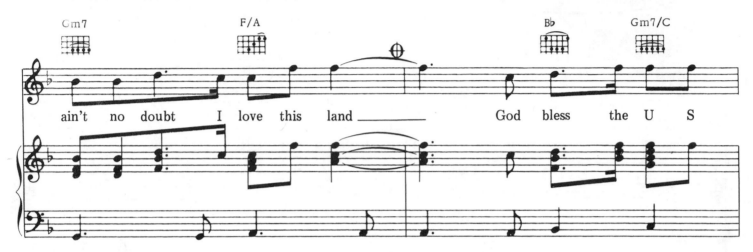

ain't no doubt I love this land _____ God bless the U S

A   (2.) From the

Verse

lakes of Min-ne-so-ta, to the hills of Ten-nes-see, _____ a-

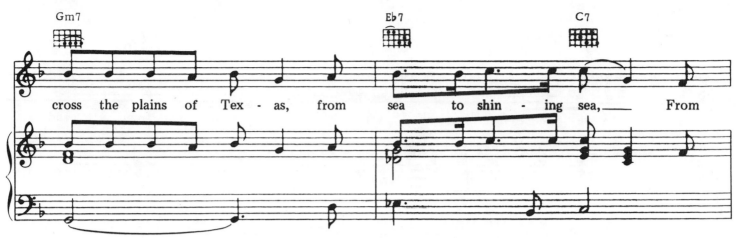

cross the plains of Tex - as, from sea to shin - ing sea,___ From

De - troit down to Hous - ton and New York to L A Well, there's

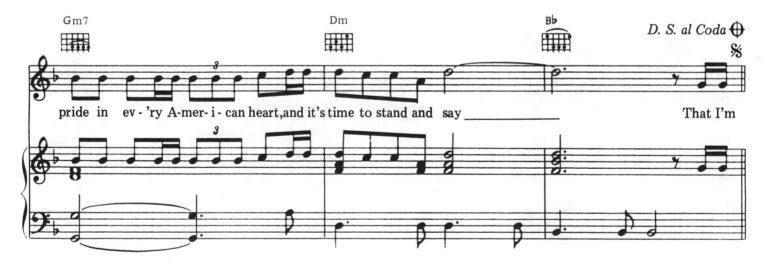

pride in ev - 'ry A-mer- i - can heart, and it's time to stand and say _____ That I'm

D. S. al Coda

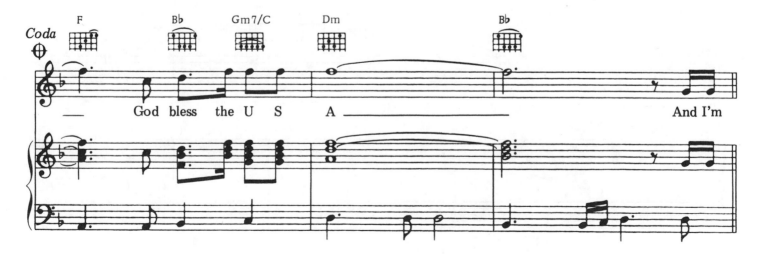

Coda

___ God bless the U S A _____ And I'm

22

proud to be an A-mer-i-can___ where at least I know I'm free, and I

won't for-get the men who died, who gave that right to me. And I'd glad-ly

stand up next to you, and de-fend her still to-day. 'Cause there

ain't no doubt I love this land ___ God bless the U S A ___

I.O.U.

Words and Music by
AUSTIN ROBERTS & KERRY CHATER

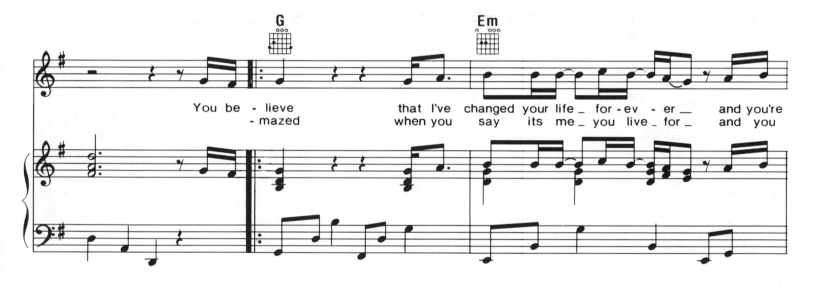

GOING GOING GONE

Words and Music by
JAN CRUTCHFIELD

Moderately Slow

Lyrics (verse 1 / verse 2):

It's o-ver, / o-ver,

I left the door un- / I nev-er thought I'd

locked a-gain, / see this day

but this time some-one new walked in / when ev'-ry-thing would walk

walked in a-way / walk a-way

while she was all a-lone. / that I de-pend-ed on.

God, he'll / He

Chord symbols: Eb, Ab, Eb, Ab, Gm, Ab, Dbmaj7, Bb

I DON'T MIND THE THORNS
(WHEN YOU'RE THE ROSE)

Words and Music by JAN BUCKINGHAM
and LINDA YOUNG

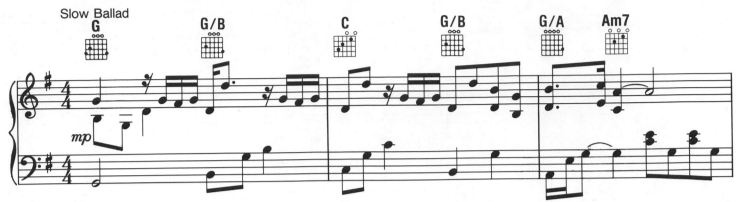

33

IT SHOULD HAVE BEEN LOVE BY NOW

Words and Music by JAN CRUTCHFIELD
and PAUL HARRISON

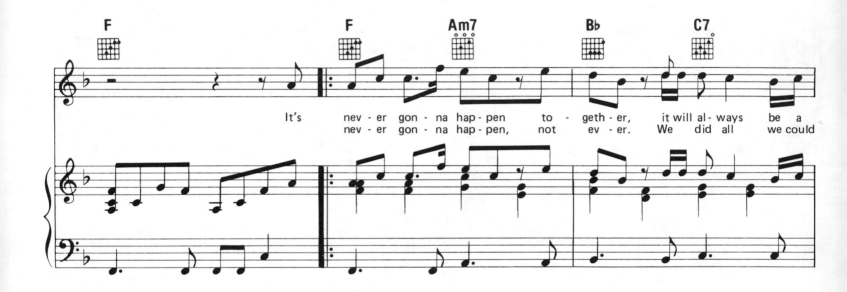

It's nev-er gon-na hap-pen to-geth-er, it will al-ways be a
nev-er gon-na hap-pen, not ev-er. We did all we could

dream.
do.

And we've tried to make it so good, and it's
You've al-ways been there for me, and I've

IT TURNS ME INSIDE OUT

Words and Music by
JAN CRUTCHFIELD

MCA MUSIC

(I FOUND) LOVE IN TIME

Words and Music by GLEN BALLARD
and CLIF MAGNESS

41

A LOVE SONG

Words and Music by
LEE GREENWOOD

MCA MUSIC

RING ON HER FINGER, TIME ON HER HANDS

Words and Music by DON GOODMAN, MARY ANN KENNEDY & PAM ROSE

49

SHE'S LYING

Words and Music by
JAN CRUTCHFIELD

MCA MUSIC

SOMEBODY'S GONNA LOVE YOU

Words and Music by RAFE VanHOY
and DON COOK

STREAMLINE

Words and Music by LEWIS ANDERSON
and BRENT MASON

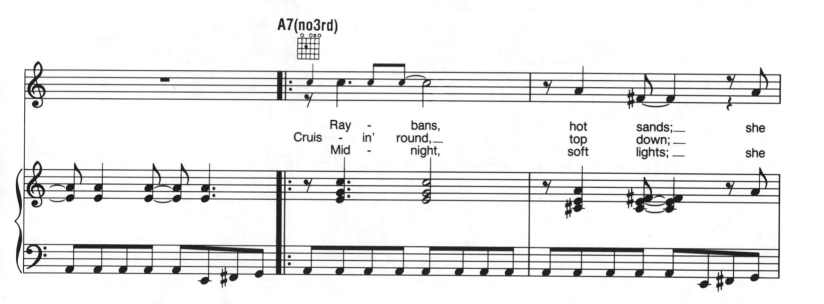

Ray - bans, hot sands; — she
Cruis - in' round, — top down; — she
Mid - night, soft lights; — she

spreads her beach towel be - side me. Got her Vogue mag - a - zine in her hair, —
no place spe - cial to go. Got the wind
pulls me out on the dance floor; with her long silk - y curls, —

TO ME

Words and Music by MACK DAVID
and MIKE REID

THE WIND BENEATH MY WINGS

Words and Music by
LARRY HENLEY and JEFF SILBAR

It must have been cold ___ there ___ in my shad - ow, ___
I was the one ___ with ___ all the glo - ry ___

to nev - er have the sun - light on your
while you were the one with all the

You've been con - tent ___
On - ly a face

face.
strength.

YOU'VE GOT A GOOD LOVE COMIN'

Words and Music by DANNY MORRISON,
VAN STEPHENSON and JEFF SILBAR